Panther and Frog

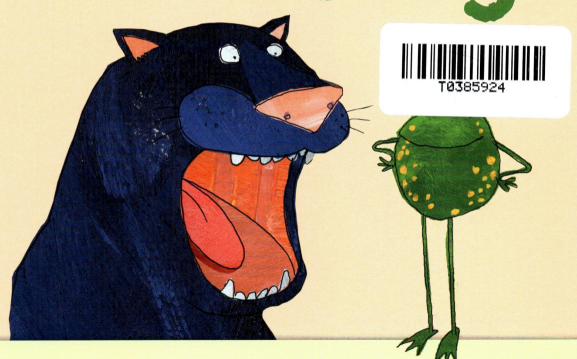

Written by Paul Shipton
Illustrated by Lee Wildish

Panther is big and strong, and all the animals are afraid of him.

All but Frog ...

"Run!" growls Panther, but Frog just sits on a log.

"I am bigger and stronger than you!" growls Panther.
"Perhaps," croaks Frog.

"I am the best hunter," growls
Panther. "All the animals fear me!"

"Perhaps," croaks Frog.

"I can fight and hunt better than you," growls Panther.

"I can run quicker and jump higher!"
Panther jumps up high in the air.

"That was good," croaks Frog.
"But can you hop across this log?"

Frog lures Panther to the log
and hops across it.

"Yes, I can hop across this log!" thunders Panther. He starts to run, but he is too big.

The log cracks and Panther
drops into the river.

"You are bigger and stronger ... and now you are wetter!" croaks Frog.

"I will get you!" growls Panther.

"No, you will not!" Frog tells him.
"I am a better swimmer than you!"